Better Homes and Gardens®

NATURE'S GARDENS

Create a Haven for Birds,
Butterflies—and Yourself!

BETTER HOMES AND GARDENS® BOOKS
Des Moines

BETTER HOMES AND GARDENS® Books
An Imprint of Meredith® Books

NATURE'S GARDENS
Editor: Doug Jimerson
Art Director: Brad Ruppert
Writer: Karen Weir Jimerson
Senior Editor: Marsha Jahns
Copy Editors: Durrae Johanek, Mary Helen Schiltz
Photographer: Peter Krumhardt
Illustrators: Sharon Bradley Papp and Eugene Thompson
Production Manager: Douglas Johnston

Vice President and Editorial Director: Elizabeth P. Rice
Executive Editor: Kay Sanders
Art Director: Ernest Shelton
Managing Editor: Christopher Cavanaugh

President, Book Group: Joseph J. Ward
Vice President, Retail Marketing: Jamie L. Martin
Vice President, Direct Marketing: Timothy Jarrell

Meredith Corporation
Chairman of the Executive Committee: E. T. Meredith III
Chairman of the Board and Chief Executive Officer: Jack D. Rehm
President and Chief Operating Officer: William T. Kerr

All of us at Meredith® Books are dedicated to providing you with the information
and ideas you need to garden successfully. We guarantee your satisfaction with this
book for as long as you own it. If you have any questions, comments, or sugges-
tions, please write to us at:

MEREDITH® BOOKS, Garden Books
Editorial Department, RW 240
1716 Locust St.
Des Moines, IA 50309-3023

Introduction

Your backyard can become a natural gathering place for singing birds, brightly colored butterflies, and other creatures great and small. Enticing the local wildlife is easy. And it doesn't mean you have to live with the wild, unkempt look of the woods. Most plant and tree species favored by wildlife also look attractive in any landscape plan. By planting sheltering trees, berry-laden shrubs and vines, and nectar-rich flowers, you can create a yard that fulfills your own leisure needs, as well as providing a habitat for the local flora and fauna. Whatever your lot size or garden area, you can create wildlife-attractive havens through your choice of plantings. And what you cannot naturally create in your yard, you can improvise. A few well placed feeders, birdbaths, and houses in your yard, will provide wildlife with all the needed essentials of life: shelter, food, and water.

Table of Contents

Landscaping for Wildlife—Welcome wildlife to your yard by creating a haven for birds, beasts, and butterflies. Regardless of your lot size, you can create natural settings that appeal to wildlife without losing your yard to wilderness. You can share your living space with the local fauna simply by adding the food and shelter required by the type of birds, insects, and animals you want to attract. Natural food sources, such as berry-laden shrubs and vines, will entice birds and insects with a free meal. Trees offer nesting spots and cover to encourage longer visits. Add a reliable water source, and creatures great and small will call your yard home. In this chapter, you'll meet four creative gardeners who are also generous patrons of wildlife. Their gardens' largess provides home and sustenance to a rich variety of plants and animals.

SALLY GEIST

Landscaping with both people and wildlife in mind

Taming the wilderness to accommodate the needs of both wildlife and a family is a challenge. With a little more than an acre of overgrown, deeply forested backyard, Oregonian Sally Geist envisioned a garden that would play host to the local wildlife and still be usable for people. "I started out small, with only a vegetable garden and flower bed," Sally says. "Soon, however, I wanted something different. I wanted a garden that would attract my wildlife neighbors." To start, Sally created a sunny clearing by slashing through a bramble of blackberry vines and judiciously removing several towering Douglas fir trees. Next, the Geists added infrastructure and architecture. Paths, arbors, fences, and a pond all found a home in the Geist yard. Although the addition of paths and structures adds a human element to the wildlife setting, all materials were chosen for their natural color and ability to blend gracefully into the surroundings. Pots of annuals positioned along the path add early color as well as nectar for bees and butterflies.

An arched gate, right, divides the front lawn from the patio.

A key element to attracting wildlife is a reliable water source, so the Geists added a trickling waterfall as an ever-plentiful supply of drinking water for their small wild friends. "The waterfall attracts a surprising number of birds to our backyard," says Sally. "Plus we all love the sound of the water moving over the boulders." The pond is home to koi, frogs, toads, and a host of water insects who find cover amid water lilies, iris, and other aquatic plants. Birds also dip into the pond for daily refreshment. With water and food sources, their yard contains all the comforts of home.

Mixing perennial flowers and shrubs, left and above, is a good way to provide both food and cover for nearby wildlife.

Even the smallest body of water will attract frogs, right, and other aquatic creatures.

Sally fills her garden with a generous assortment of nectar-rich perennial and annual flowers, many of which she raises in her greenhouse. Cleverly tucked beneath a verdant canopy of trees, the greenhouse looks as if it grew there naturally. Old-fashioned roses cover its sides, softening the intrusion of a man-made structure in the wilderness. The snowy white rose 'Blanc Double de Coubert' bears fragrant blooms that bees find irresistible. David Austin's rose 'Gertrude Jekyll' bears large hips in the fall that birds can eat. Another vine that attracts wildlife, 'Clematis Henryii,' blooms on an arbor, offering a dizzying array of nectar-rich blooms. Windfalls from the row of espaliered dwarf apple trees provide ants, bees, and other insects with a sweet repast.

Bog plants such as the water lily, above, and the water iris, arrowhead, and marsh marigolds, right, help soften the transition between the Geists' water pond and the surrounding garden.

The caterpillar, below, of a black swallowtail butterfly prefers to dine on plants in the carrot family, such as parsley and dill.

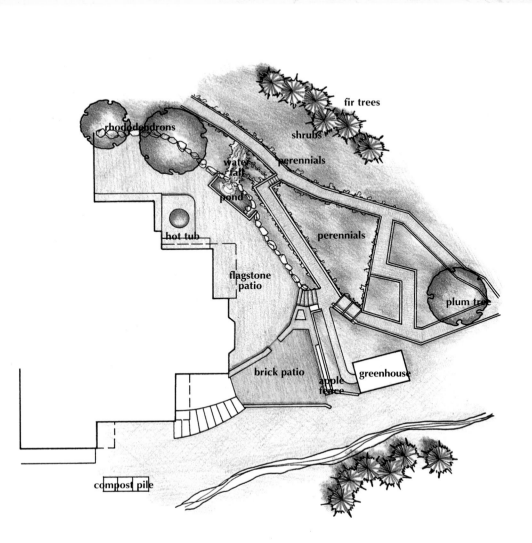

fir trees

rhododendrons

shrubs

perennials

water fall

pond

perennials

hot tub

plum tree

flagstone patio

brick patio

apple fence

greenhouse

compost pile

For the family, Sally incorporated a pair of decks to provide vantage points to watch birds and butterflies flitting from branch to fountain. "We didn't want to overlook our own needs when we designed the garden, so we built decks where we could relax and watch the action," Sally says. The yard's steep hillsides were tamed with railroad-tie terraces and planted with perennials and old-fashioned roses. A dry riverbed helps with drainage during heavy rains and creates a focal point in the yard. "The finished project is very easy to maintain. There's no lawn to mow, and the landscaping pretty much takes care of itself," Sally says. "This kind of garden would work anywhere, and the rewards are indescribable."

Sally starts many of her plants in her backyard greenhouse, right. She located the structure in the sunniest part of the yard, and then planted vines and shrubs nearby so the greenhouse would blend in with the surroundings.

Attracting birds with berried shrubs and vines

Sandwiched between a salt marsh and the sea, Pat and Jack Bowman's 3-acre New Jersey garden is a natural gathering place for local and migratory birds. Starting with a crowded, overgrown lot, Pat and Jack mapped out the spot for their home. When they cleared the land to build, the Bowmans left much of the natural vegetation intact. "I don't believe you should bulldoze everything in sight and then replace the lost vegetation with non-native species," says Pat. That meant native trees, shrubs, flowers, and vines that had been growing and providing a natural food source for neighboring species of birds were incorporated into a garden, instead of being considered wild bramble. Plants the Bowmans worked to preserve were wild cherry, red cedar, sour gum, sumac, bayberry, elderberry, holly, hawthorn, sassafras, serviceberry, dogwood, Virginia creeper, wild grape, pitch pine, and mulberry. Pat's yard proves that wildlife gardens can incorporate the human element as well. Indulging her own gardening tastes, Pat creates a spectacular mix of perennials and annuals in her front-yard flower border.

Pat's colorful perennial border, right, is a favorite spot for honeybees.

An herb garden, interplanted
with roses and perennials, is
a visual as well as literal feast
for birds and butterflies.

Islands of native vegetation throughout Pat's yard have been supplemented with domestic plants that wildlife enjoy. "Never underestimate the value of ground covers like ajuga and vinca. They provide cover for a host of insects, frogs, toads, and other critters." The abundance of shade in the Bowmans' yard provides ample space for a host of shade-loving domestic plants such as hosta, Siberian iris, vinca, astilbe, daylily, azalea, ajuga, and crocosmia. Pat chooses both native and domestic plants that provide a mixed variety of food throughout the year. To encourage wildlife visitors year-round, she also keeps bird feeders fully stocked from November through April. "Early spring is probably the most critical time to feed the birds because by then natural food supplies are low." An avid beekeeper, Pat makes sure there is a constant source of nectar-producing plants to keep her busy bees happy and well fed. Because Pat has several acres to work with, she has created mini habitats for different types of wildlife.

What was once a tangle of underbrush, left, is now a bird-pleasing assortment of domestic and wild plants. Pat has planned the garden so there's something for birds to eat in every season. Monarch butterflies, above, love buddleia.

Although a stone's throw from the ocean, Pat's property has two freshwater sources: a pond and a side-yard water garden. The pond, not an original feature to the property, was formerly a low-lying wet spot. The Bowmans dug out the area and allowed the pond to form naturally. Surrounded by heavy overgrowth that provides home and cover for birds and insects, the pond is the centerpiece to the "wild" area habitat of the Bowman yard. It's also stocked with bass and sunfish that her son, Lance, above, enjoys catching on lazy summer afternoons. Maintaining natural species was a primary goal when creating the yard plan. "Whenever possible we left every tree, even the dead ones, intact—there's so much habitat built into a dead tree," Pat says. In fact, one of her favorite trees has been dead for several years. "The dead sour gum tree that sits next to our pond probably attracts more birds than any other tree in the yard," she says.

In the fall, a wide assortment of bird species uses the Bowmans' freshwater pond, right, as a rest stop on their migration south.

The Bowmans created a small pond by digging out a low-lying wet spot. Now the pond attracts birds and insects that otherwise might not visit. To add summer color, Pat has both tropical and hardy water lilies.

Pat's secluded side-yard water garden provides a habitat for frogs, toads, fish, and insects. Planted with a smorgasbord of domestic, native, and aquatic plants, it also makes good use of an awkward spot beside her house. The long, narrow pool hosts exotic water plants such as water lily, cattail, miniature cattail, and pickerel weed. Pat worked to create a hospitable place for her wildlife visitors, one that's shaded and well sheltered. Animals can feast on violet, iris, lily, hydrangea, rose, ornamental grasses, lamb's ears, rosemary, daylily, rudbeckia, coreopsis, and nigella. Also found in this small side-yard garden are dragon's blood sedum, monarda, ajuga, liriope, catmint, honeysuckle, Bradford pear, Korean lilac, smokebush, and winter jasmine. By planting the way nature does, Pat makes the most of her small space. "Take a cue from Mother Nature and plant your garden in vertical layers. Use ground covers on the bottom level, shrubs for understory, and trees for canopy," Pat says.

Pat's side-yard garden, opposite, proves that you don't have to have a large acreage to create a wonderful wildlife garden. In this tiny strip of land, Pat has included an amazing array of flowers, ground covers, bulbs, and herbs, along with a water garden and a vine-covered entry trellis. The overall garden plan for Pat's garden, right, shows how many mini habitats she's created in one yard.

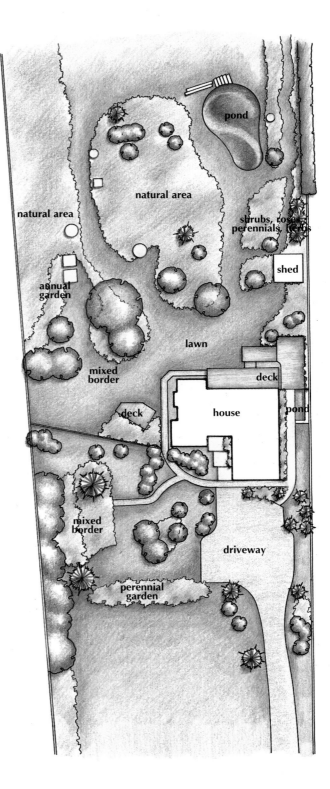

MEG & JACQUES ST. LOUIS

Transforming a problem lot into a bird-watcher's paradise

After building their home on a precipitous Oregon hillside, Meg and Jacques St. Louis turned their sights to making their backyard a place they could go as a family to eat, to relax, and to enjoy one another's company. "What backyard?" Jacques jokes. "This lot looked more like a ski run!" Because the family was more interested in bird-watching than skiing, they embarked on a yard renovation. Undaunted by the restrictions of their vertical landscape, the St. Louis family took the first step in any good yard design—they each cast their vote on what type of outdoor living space they wanted. Jacques envisioned a restful brook trickling down the slope and spilling into a small pond filled with brightly colored koi. Meg and the children are avid bird-watchers, so they wanted to preserve the hillside ecology and enhance its bird-attracting potential by adding well-stocked feeders and plants that provide natural food sources. In addition, they all wanted places to eat and relax.

The St. Louises' sloping backyard, right, was carefully designed to make the most out of what had been a problem lot.

Before they could build their spacious multilevel deck, the St. Louis family had to solve some essential structural problems. Good drainage on the steep hillside was essential to prevent mudslides into the back of the house. To remedy the problem, Meg and Jacques hauled heavy rocks up the hillside, one at a time by pulley, from the street far below to form the streambed and waterfall. "We really did feel like we were moving mountains at times," Meg says. With unflagging persistence, however, the St. Louis family carved out their wildlife retreat in just one season. To preserve the natural beauty of their slope, the St. Louises chiseled out just enough space for a multilevel deck. Planters and benches hold the hill in place by doubling as retaining walls.

Feeders placed strategically around the St. Louises' back-yard, left, lure birds like the house finch, above.

Because attracting birds was a family objective for the landscape design, the St. Louises planted a rich abundance of ground covers, in which hungry birds can forage for insects. Ivies and ferns cover the hillside and pull double duty as vegetative resistance to any drainage problems. Bird feeders also encourage local and migratory birds to descend. Meg's movable feeders, suspended from wires between the trees to protect them from predators, also attract bluebirds, doves, house wrens, grosbeaks, goldfinches, house finches, Western meadowlarks, and, on occasion, orioles. By keeping feeders filled in autumn through late spring, the St. Louises ensure a host of bird species will continue to call their yard home. Birds also find the tall trees a perfect nesting habitat. The backyard stream was included as a water source for local birds. A recirculating pump keeps the water moving, thus preventing stagnancy problems. Containers and planters are stocked with annuals that entice butterflies and hummingbirds.

Nectar-rich annuals such as zinnia, cosmos, or tithonia, right, start attracting butterflies as soon as their buds begin to open. Tiger swallowtails, below, love zinnias, especially the single-flowered varieties like 'Cut 'n' Come Again.' Ground covers and herbs, above, ramble through stones in the garden.

The key to the St. Louises' success is
that their yard mimics the nearby forests
of the Pacific Northwest. Clumps of ivy,
ferns, and rhododendron thrive on the
back slope beneath stands of Douglas fir,
alder, and maple trees. The backyard
stream is attractive to all sorts of wildlife,
with water lilies and other aquatic
beauties planted in sunken pots set into
the 40-inch-deep pond. Just 10 feet
across at its widest point, the pond is
home to koi, goldfish, frogs, snails, and
insects. The vinyl-lined streambed
stair-steps down the slope and looks as
if Mother Nature had laid the stones
herself. A recirculating pump, hidden
from view, keeps the water flowing and
clear at all times. Because the plantings
are designed to surround the deck, the
St. Louises relax in their outdoor retreat
with the sights and sounds of nature.
Chirping finches and chickadees,
fluttering hummingbirds, splashing
water, and children's laughter
intermingle to create an environment
where people and animals live together
in harmony.

**The St. Louises' backyard, opposite and right, shows how a
"hopeless" lot can be transformed into a handsome refuge
for both people and animals. Drainage and erosion problems also are solved by planting a variety of ground covers,
shrubs, and understory trees.**

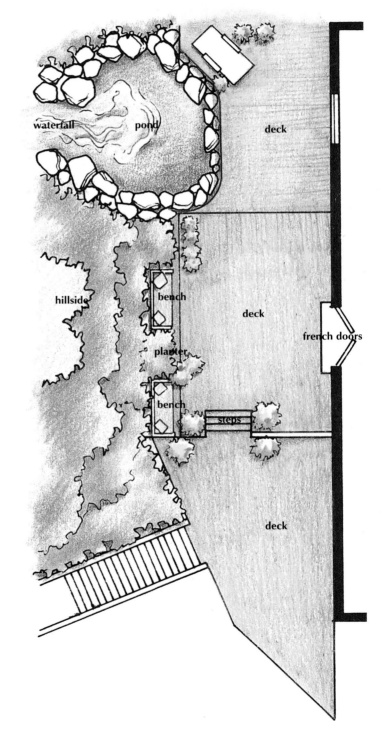

Using native plants to create an easy-care garden

Frank Nykiel had ulterior motives when he designed his garden. Frank's goal was to create an outdoor getaway that would help take the edge off his high-powered workday as a corporate consultant. The result, however, was a wildlife retreat, complete with native plants, lily pond, and a host of colorful annuals and perennials. Frank's desire for a stress-free garden culminated in a selection of plants that can fend for themselves through Missouri's steamy-hot summers and bitter-cold winters. "It had to be undemanding. Because I had a high-risk job, the last thing I wanted was a high-risk garden," says Frank. Summing up his planting philosophy, Frank states simply: "I just plant stuff that won't die." The core of his garden is a mixture of hardy native wildflowers and tough, drought-resistant perennials. Plants that are indigenous to the region and accustomed to the climate and soil type are foolproof choices. Plus, natives are a natural food source for wildlife.

The family cat, right, is lured into the Nykiel garden for a drink from the lily pond. It's a good idea to attach a bell to a cat's collar to warn birds that a cat is near.

The pair of arbors that flank Frank's garden, left, provide architectural interest and support for summer-flowering vines such as honeysuckle and trumpet vine.

Robins, right, are just one species of bird that nest near Frank's garden.

All visitors to the Nykiel garden (whether walking in or flying through for a look) are welcomed in grand style by a rustic wooden archway. To separate the garden from the surrounding cropland, Frank chose wooden fencing that weathered to a natural gray. Climbing vines (such as grape, which provides berries, and trumpet vine, which produces flowers), along with the plantings of native and perennial flowers, provide food sources, resting spots, and shelter for birds, butterflies, and insects. Low-growing verbena, thyme, veronica, and coreopsis spill over the brick paths, offering a habitat for insects. Keep in mind that not all insects cause damage to a garden. If an infestation threatens, there are a host of nontoxic controls that are safe for the environment (and also safe for the indigenous wildlife). Releasing predatory insects, such as ladybugs, praying mantises, and lacewings is one way to keep things in balance. The best defense against marauding pests is a healthy garden. Fit plants are rarely bothered by disease or insects.

Frank's daughters Lyndsey and
Sydney discover new things on
a daily basis in the garden.
"They make decisions and take
responsibility for mistakes,"
says Frank about their partici-
pation in gardening.

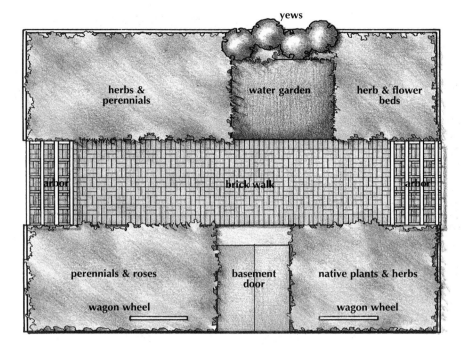

yews

herbs &
perennials

water garden

herb & flower
beds

arbor

brick walk

arbor

perennials & roses

basement
door

native plants & herbs

wagon wheel

wagon wheel

By design, Frank's flower garden spills from its fenced enclosure into the yard that surrounds the century-old Nykiel home. To attract a variety of birds and insects, the garden boasts a large diversity of plant types. Heat-loving yarrow, statice, shasta daisy, and rudbeckia flank the old cellar doors. Climbing roses, which produce tasty hips in the fall, clamber up antique wagon wheels. Care-free and hardy, coreopsis and salvia bloom across the path. By planting masses of different species and colors of flowers together, Frank attracts a wide array of birds and butterflies. Wildlife gardens are, by their nature, kind to the earth. Frank takes earth-wise gardening a step further, however, by improving the soil so new plants don't have to struggle in the clay-based Missouri soil. He also mulches generously to conserve water. And, because much of the garden is planted with native species, Frank doesn't have to fertilize or otherwise chemically enhance his plants. Avoiding wildlife-harming pesticides and herbicides is the best way for Frank to ensure that the native wildlife now inhabiting his garden will grow and prosper.

Once established, a garden like Frank Nykiel's, top, requires very little maintenance. The beds against his house, left, are filled with no-nonsense plants like coreopsis, coneflower, and yarrow.

CHAPTER TWO

Planting for Wildlife—Planting a wide variety of trees, shrubs, vines, ground covers, and flowers is the key to attracting the most wildlife to your yard. Plantings need to provide the essential foundations of life: food and shelter. Flowering and fruit-bearing trees and shrubs offer nesting areas, a haven from predators and weather, and a meal at every turn. Insects that birds thrive on live among vines and ground covers. Native plants produce nectar, seeds, and housing for wildlife of all types. And domestic flowers are a colorful repast for many wildlife species. By orchestrating diverse habitats in your backyard, you will create a landscape that is beautiful to your eye and one that you can share with all creatures great and small.

Trees are essential in every wildlife garden

Trees are the backbone of any wildlife garden. From the mightiest oak to slender understory species, trees provide nesting spots, cover from predators, shelter from inclement weather, and a smorgasbord of enticing treats. The wider the variety of tree species you plant in your yard, the larger the variety of habitats and food you'll offer to birds, insects, and other desirable garden visitors. Large trees such as oak, maple, hackberry, beech, and hickory provide shelter and nesting sites for birds, squirrels, and small mammals. Plant flowering and fruit-bearing species to provide a multiseason food feast. These trees produce nectar in the spring, nesting cover in the summer, fruit in the autumn, and shelter in the winter. Spring-blooming ornamental trees include redbud, dogwood, pear, flowering crab, acacia, horse chestnut, hawthorn, and tulip tree. Fruit trees such as apple, peach, cherry, plum, and others also should be included in your wildlife garden. Summer-flowering trees include crape myrtle, golden-rain tree, golden-chain tree, silk tree, Japanese tree lilac, and catalpa. Evergreens such as junipers and holly produce berries that mature in August and September and remain on the plant for several months.

Kousa dogwoods, right, bloom in early summer. The large, cream-colored flowers are a good food source for insects and birds.

Flowering dogwoods, above, are a wonderful addition to any landscape because they're as attractive to people as they are to your wildlife neighbors. Dogwoods develop spectacular flowers in the spring that are followed by bird-tempting berries in the summer. In the fall the foliage turns bright yellow, and during the winter the plants' graceful horizontal branches add interest to the winter landscape.

Oak and sugar maple trees, opposite, are two species you should try to include in your wildlife garden. Unfortunately, both species grow too large for small lots. Where space is limited, consider planting some of their more compact relatives. Amur maple, paperbark maple, columnar Norway maple, hedge maple, and upright English oak are all good substitutes for more space-demanding varieties.

Let Mother Nature be your guide when you plant trees in a bare backyard or add trees to an established landscape. If you study any natural setting, you'll see that trees grow in layers. Larger trees work in unison with shorter, understory species to provide a complete habitat that birds and other animals rely on. This naturally occurring layered look is easy to duplicate. Flowering trees, such as dogwood, redbud, and serviceberry, grow well under the light shade produced by taller species such as oak, maple, ash, and hickory. Pecans, walnuts, buckeyes, horse chestnuts, and butternuts are other excellent additions to your wildlife garden. Birds, squirrels, and chipmunks will live in and around these trees, feasting on their tasty harvest of nuts.

DOGWOOD

RED CEDAR

AMUR MAPLE

SOUR GUM

Native trees that bear edible wild fruits also attract wildlife. Most of these flower in the spring, providing a food source for bees, butterflies, and other insects. In midsummer, these same trees produce fruit. Serviceberry, for example, blooms in the early spring with nectar-rich flowers. By midsummer, the flowers have transformed themselves into small red and purple berries that ripen just in time for young fruit-loving robins as they leave the nest. Those berries that are not gobbled up in the summer dry naturally on the plant to provide a vitamin-rich winter food source. Crab apples and wild apples also bloom in the spring, followed by rosy-red fruits that are sour to the human palate but a treat for avian gourmets. Another tree that produces midsummer fare is the mulberry. It's a favorite of many bird species, but don't plant it near your deck or patio because the berries that fall to the ground will stain. Red cedar provides food and shelter for a wide variety of birds and animals. In the fall, its bright blue berries are especially prized by migrating songbirds, such as robins and waxwings. And because the plant is evergreen, birds can take shelter whatever the weather. Domestic fruit trees such as apple, pear, cherry, and plum develop fruit that is as appealing to wildlife as it is to people. When you plant a tree, keep in mind that it will be a permanent fixture. Consider the tree's mature size and shape before planting; don't locate it where it will eventually become a problem.

If you want instant landscaping, buy plants in large containers or balled-and-burlapped stock. Look for healthy plants that are not wilted or yellowed. Cheap plants aren't always a bargain.

Bare-root trees require immediate planting and plenty of water to get established. Soak roots in a bucket before planting. Separate the roots when you plant so they'll get off to a good start.

If you have more patience than money, seedlings are a good way to add trees and shrubs to your landscape because you can buy large quantities inexpensively.

Shrubs are the backbone of every wildlife garden

Most shrubs found at your local nursery are also wildlife friendly. Low-growing species with thorny branches such as barberry offer birds both a meal and a safe place to eat. Taller species, like the viburnums, which produce a variety of red and purple berries, are popular with landscapers because they work well in most gardens. The cold-hardy arrowwood viburnum grows 10 to 15 feet tall and bears small white flowers in the spring, which are attractive in the landscape as well as to insects and butterflies. In the autumn, the shrub yields glossy, blue-black berries that provide nourishment for hungry songbirds. Even the decorative snowball viburnum, which produces fragrant, white, ball-shaped flowers in late spring and red bunches of berries in the fall, appeals to wildlife. Able to withstand harsh winters, this shrub is both an attractive landscape planting and a multiseason food source for wildlife. The most colorful member of the viburnum family, cranberry bush or highbush cranberry, exhibits nectar-rich, 2- to 3-inch clusters of white flowers in the spring and vibrant red berries in the fall.

Forsythia and rhododendron, right, offer lots of color in the early spring and are a welcome food source for insects.

Another popular landscape plant is cotoneaster, a versatile shrub with species that spread across the ground or grow erect to heights of 15 feet. Evergreen and producing ruby-colored berries, cotoneaster shines as a beautiful landscaping species as well as for the interest it draws from passing birds. To attract the largest number and variety of wildlife species, plant a variety of shrubs that bear fruit at different times during the late summer and fall. Autumn olive is a favorite with migratory birds because its juicy berries ripen in mid-September, just when the birds need a high-energy snack. In January and February, overwintering species find the plant's orange-scarlet berries a needed feast. This winter-hardy shrub grows 6 feet tall, and it's easily trained to grow up a trellis or the side of your house.

In the fall, beautyberry, above, develops scores of small, pinkish-purple fruit. Weigela, opposite, is a good choice for early spring flowers.

oriole

Roses, too, are a good source of food for birds during the winter. Rose species such as *Rosa eglanteria*, the sweetbrier rose, and rugosa roses produce hips after the flowers fade in the fall. Rose hips are rich in vitamins and are relished by robins, waxwings, and bluebirds. Shrub roses also provide a summer nesting habitat for many birds and cover for overwintering songbirds. Another appealing shrub is the elderberry, which grows to 12 feet tall and provides natural cover for the birds that feast on its juicy midsummer berries. Honeysuckle shrubs grow to 10 feet tall. Depending on the species, they flower in pink, yellow, or white, and produce red or crimson fruit. Other shrubs that bear fruit include dogwood, currant, gooseberry, blueberry, and holly.

In a shrub border you can't beat any of the spring-blooming spireas, left. Honeysuckle, above, produces both flowers and fruit that birds find irresistible.

VIBURNUM

DOGWOOD

CRANBERRY BUSH

As with trees, the greater diversity of shrubs you plant, the larger the number of wildlife visitors you'll entice into your yard. Another advantage of planting several shrub species is that it protects your wildlife garden from total plant loss as a result of disease or insects. For best results, mix low-, medium-, and tall-growing species together to create a habitat for birds at different levels. This natural, layered planting plan accommodates all types of wildlife species, from underground dwellers to those who own the skies. By choosing shrub species that provide food for all seasons, birds also will seek out your yard year-round. In addition to the songbirds and game birds, fruit-bearing shrubs will entice small animals such as rabbits, chipmunks, and squirrels into your garden. Once planted, most shrubs require little or no care. An occasional pruning will keep most species in bounds. If you have oversize shrubs, you can often rejuvenate them with a severe pruning in the early spring. Dogwood, honeysuckle, and lilac benefit from pruning.

Robins and other fruit-loving birds will flock to your yard when the serviceberries' tasty fruit, right, begins to ripen. Generally, the fruit is ready to eat in late June or early July. Space serviceberries about 6 feet apart.

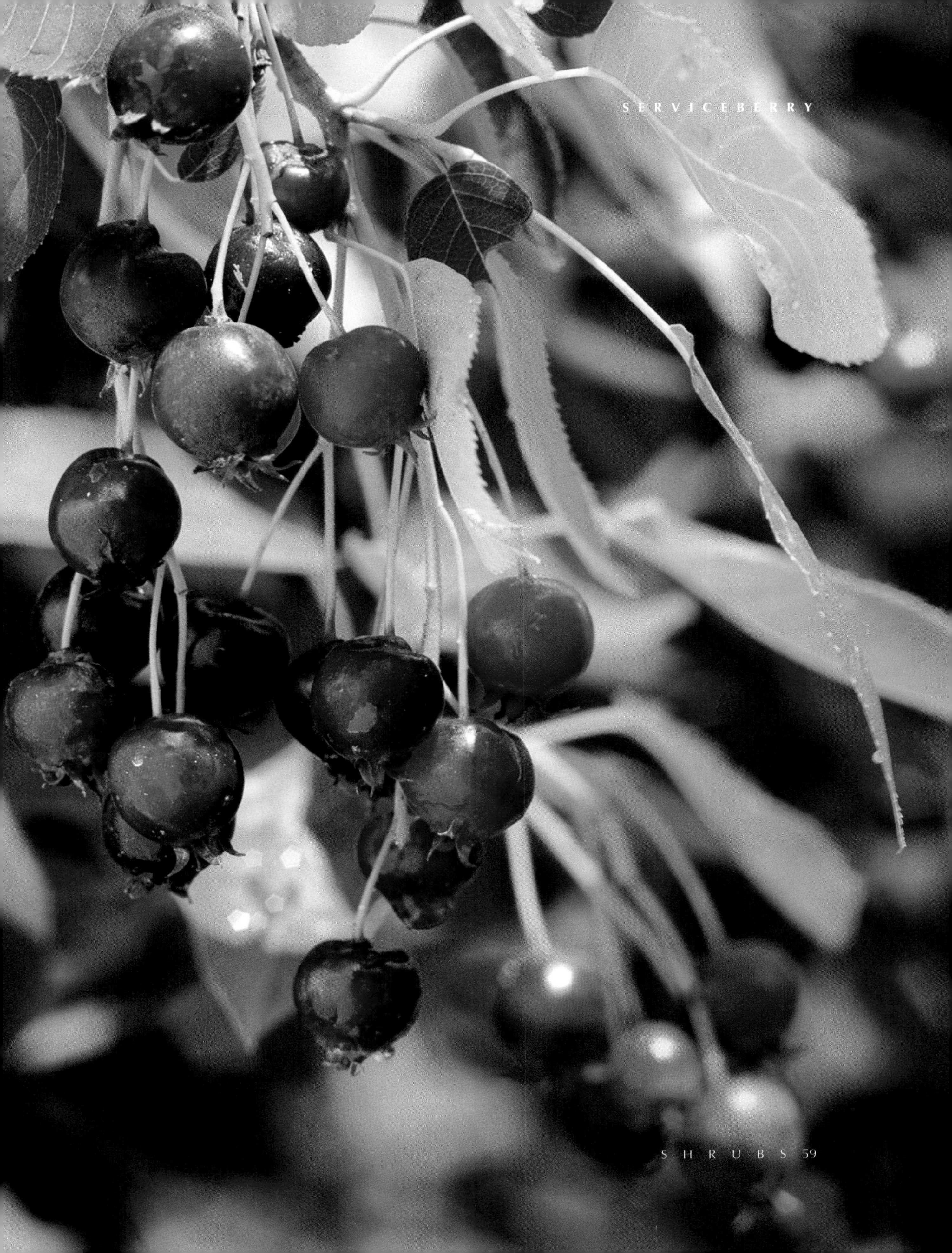

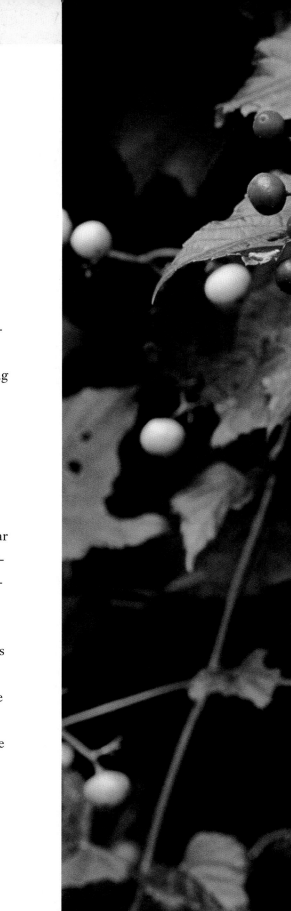

Vines offer food and shelter for birds of all types

No wildlife garden is complete without a generous help-ing of vines. Tumbling over arbors, scrambling up rock walls, or winding their way through large trees, flowering vines are showy centerpieces to any landscape. Most vines also lure butterflies, birds, and bees, who find the nectar-rich blossoms irresistible. Vines accommodate many wildlife needs. Perennial vines such as Virginia creeper, trumpet vine, and Boston ivy offer food and cover for a wide assortment of wildlife. In late summer, the colorful marblelike fruit of porcelain vine is a popular food source for birds. In some parts of the country, how-ever, porcelain vine can become invasive. Virginia creep-er berries appeal to wildlife later in the winter, when other sources are most scarce. In the summer, you can satisfy the sweet tooth of hummingbirds and bumblebees by planting trumpet vine. Its orange-red, nectar-rich flowers appear from June until August. Sun-loving grape species growing along fences will create nesting cover and bear summer fruits on which birds will feast. Be sure to plant plenty of grapevines so that both you and the birds can enjoy their fruit.

Fast growing and attractive, porcelain vine, right, is ideal where you need quick cover to camouflage an eyesore.

Trumpet vine is a valuable addition to the diet of hummingbirds and bumblebees. These vigorous vines can grow 30 feet long, so be sure to give the plants plenty of elbow room. A strong trellis is also essential so the plants don't topple in high winds.

Another perennial wildlife pleaser is honeysuckle vine, which bears fragrant flowers in the spring and berries from July through September. This fast-growing vine has dense foliage that provides protection for the birds, which love its red fruit. Unlike honeysuckle, which requires full sun, Boston ivy will thrive in partial shade, bearing bird-tempting berries in the late summer. Another perennial vine, Dutchman's pipe is attractive to some caterpillar species. Climbing roses are another option if you want a colorful plant for a trellis or arbor. Besides their flowers, many species of climbing roses produce tasty, vitamin-rich hips. Some annual vines, such as morning glory, black-eyed Susan vine, cardinal climber, scarlet runner bean, and moon flower, also are used by birds for nesting sites and late-summer snacks. These species grow quickly from seed and offer cover while slower-growing perennial vines take hold.

The dense foliage and fragrant flowers of wisteria, left, provide food and shelter for a variety of insects and birds. For wildlife viewing close up, train climbing roses around a window, above, or a doorway.

After frost, your annual vines will die back, but you can leave the withered flowers and foliage in place so birds can harvest the seeds. Combining both annual and perennial vine species in your landscape is a surefire way to encourage the neighboring wildlife to drop in. Vines, while home for many insect and bird species, also are an important food source for other wildlife. Virginia creeper, bittersweet, grape, and wisteria all develop some type of tasty treat on which squirrels, opossums, raccoons, foxes, and rabbits depend. The fruit that forms on these vines is at its best from late summer to early winter, a time when these animals need an extra dose of energy. In Northern states, bird species that don't migrate also depend on these winter food sources. Nuthatches, chickadees, downy and hairy woodpeckers, cardinals, blue jays, house finches and goldfinches, titmice, and waxwings are just some species that benefit when you include these winter-bearing vines in your garden plan.

Actinidia kolomikta, **right, is hardy enough to grow in sun or shade. The foliage of this relatively rare climber is pink and white. Because it grows 20 feet tall, use a sturdy trellis to keep the plant from toppling. Mourning doves, below, often nest in thick vines.**

Use ground covers generously in your wildlife garden

Amid the dense foliage of ground-cover plantings exists a tiny world shielded from most inquiring human eyes. Hidden beneath the canopy of these ground-hugging plants scurry beetles, grubs, spiders, ladybugs, and other insects, most of which insect-eating birds happily feast upon. Toads and frogs are also at home in the lush undergrowth of ground-cover plants. By planting ground covers, you'll not only create havens for smaller wildlife, but you'll also add an important finishing touch to your land-scape. Revered for their tenacious growth habits, ground covers are the easy answer to hard landscape problems. There are ground-cover species that thrive in sunny or shady conditions. Used to soften and fill in barren areas of your yard, ground covers provide color and texture in places that need it most—under trees and taller plantings, for example. By turning over part of your lawn to ground covers, you'll spend less time mowing and more time watch-ing the birds attracted to the rich abundance of food sources that live among the lush leaves of ground covers.

A mass planting of 'Beacon Silver' lamium, left, helps hold this sloping garden in place during heavy rains. Lamium, which is occasionally called dead nettle, grows 6 to 8 inches tall.

Perennial ground covers are hardy growers, spreading more each year. These care-free plants come in varieties that grow in all light and soil conditions. Their soil-holding root systems make them excellent plantings on slopes, where erosion is a problem. Perennial ground covers that are especially wildlife friendly include ajuga, honeysuckle, pachysandra, and vinca. Ajuga bears bright blue flower spires in spring and has lovely textured foliage the rest of the summer. The nectar-rich, spring-blooming, honeysuckle ground cover is an enticement to insects of all kinds. Honeysuckle offers fall berries, which are a favorite of birds, as well. Both pachysandra and vinca also offer hiding places in their dense leaves.

Many ground covers look their best growing in the dense shade provided by tall trees. In this garden, right, ferns and forget-me-nots thrive. White-crowned sparrows, top, feed on the ground.

In the spring, vinca produces wave after wave of deep blue flowers that insects rely on as an early food source. A hardy perennial, vinca can carpet a shady spot in just a few years. Unlike some ground covers, vinca never loses its leaves, even in cold Northern gardens.

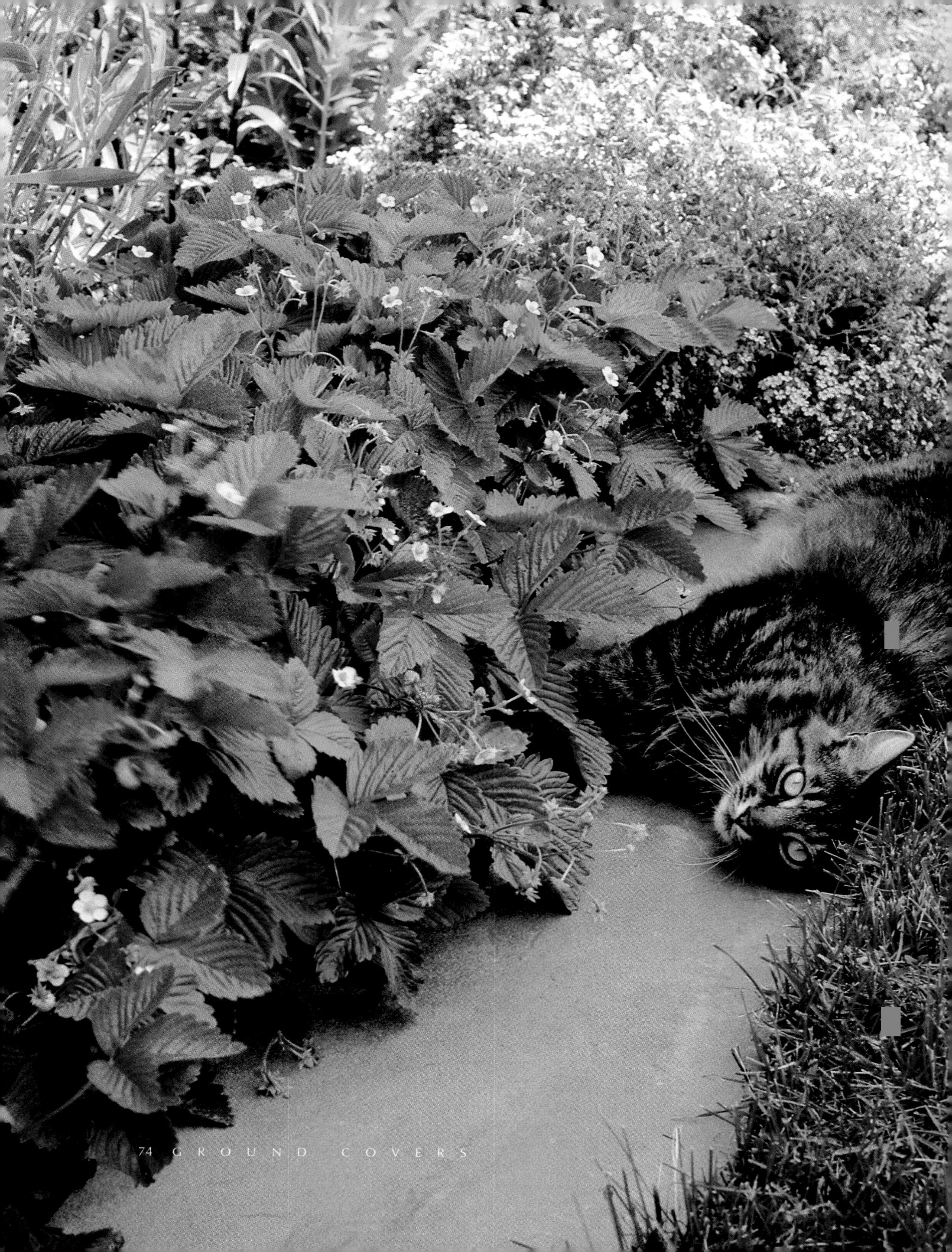

Another fruit-bearing ground cover is alpine strawberry, which produces sweet berries for songbirds like waxwings and robins. Other perennial ground covers that entice wildlife include buttercup, ivy, and a host of low-growing herbs, such as thyme and sweet woodruff. While your perennial ground covers become established, use annual ground covers such as sweet alyssum, verbena, and portulaca to fill in the spaces. Annual ground covers also include creeping varieties of flowers such as petunia and phlox. Colorful and nectar rich, these plants provide food and cover for a minute world of insects. To create the most natural look, avoid setting ground-cover plants in straight rows. For quick coverage, buy lots of plants and set them close together. Or, buy fewer plants, space them farther apart, and allow them to fill in naturally over time. Most species grow best when planted 1 foot apart. Set tall ferns or more vigorous plants 2 feet apart.

Alpine strawberries, opposite, and 'Pink Panda' strawberries, top right, are both good choices for birds. Anole lizards, right, live on the garden floor.

NATIVES

Rely on native plants to attract your wildlife neighbors

Native plantings are especially good for attracting local wildlife, because these plants are the original diet of the species in your area. They're also easy to grow because they're naturally accustomed to your climate, soil type, and moisture levels. Once established, most native plants and weeds require little coddling, often surviving in locations where other plant species fail. Insects, birds, and other animals rely on native plants for most of their dietary needs. Bees, for example, gather nectar from hundreds of different types of wild plants. Sweet clover, fruit trees, basswood, wild raspberries, and sage are just a few of their favorites. Butterflies also look to natives as a food source for themselves and their young. Monarch caterpillars, for example, need milkweed leaves to survive.

Purple coneflower, black-eyed Susan, and false dragonhead, right, create a banquet of bloom when planted in masses.

Queen butterfly

Planted together, zinnias and black-eyed Susans are an irresistible lure for a wide assortment of insects.

Native plants are as at home in a cultivated garden as they are growing in the ditches and fields of the countryside. Domestic versions of wildflowers are equally interesting to wildlife. Species found in the wild, which also have domestic siblings, are yarrow, coneflowers, and aster. Both the wild and the cultivated forms of yarrow attract insects birds can eat. Butterfly weed will provide a banquet of bugs for insect-eating birds. You can tuck a few natives into your existing garden, or, if you have the space, let part of your yard go native with wildings such as milkweed, wild yarrow, nettle, and butterfly weed.

Butterfly weed, opposite, tolerates hot, dry conditions. Plant it in a sunny location where the plant will prosper and butterflies will find it. In shady gardens, above, mayapple and bleeding heart thrive.

If you have a lot of space, you can plant a prairie garden with native grasses and wildflowers. Your state's Department of Natural Resources will be able to give you guidelines for the species that originally grew in your area. In addition to the food your local wildlife can harvest, prairie plantings also provide nesting sites for birds such as meadow larks, pheasants, and quail. Other weeds and native plants that appeal to a wild menagerie include: clover, Queen Anne's lace, goldenrod, fleabane, spiderwort, poke weed, bee-balm, black-eyed Susan, mullein, blue vervain, catnip, common plantain, Joe-Pye weed, wild sunflower, oxeye daisy, thistle, and nettle.

Combine shade-loving domestic and wild plants under tall trees to create a haven for people and wildlife. Hosta, bleeding heart, and fern, left, are a winning combination.

Flowers add color, fragrance, and beauty to every wildlife garden

The same elements that attract you to a beautiful garden also bring in wildlife: continuous bloom, color, and fragrance. By planting a mix of perennial and annual flowers that provide a spring-to-fall supply of bloom, you'll not only have a lush and verdant garden, but also an endless feast for bees, butterflies, and birds. Because insects are attracted to different hues, plant a broad range of flower colors. The more flower varieties you have in your garden, the more insect and bird species will seek out your yard as a refuge. Always plant annual and perennial flowers in masses so you have a large buffet for out-of-town guests. Perennials provide a sense of permanence to your yard in the same way trees and shrubs do. The wildlife that are attracted to these plants will be return visitors each year to partake in the feast these flowers offer. For gardeners, perennials are also popular because of their easy care and hardy nature. Perennials are available in a wide array of species and in all heights and flowering times, so it's simple to orchestrate a garden that stays in full bloom from spring through fall. Just be sure to plant species that are adaptable to your climate.

Hosta, hydrangea, snakeroot, iris, and lady's mantle are just a few of the perennial flowers in this sun-and-shade border, right.

Birds and butterflies aren't fussy about the type of garden they visit, as long as an assortment of food plants is available. This garden is popular with animals because it contains perennials and annuals

Perennial species that are particularly attractive to wildlife include bee-balm, poppy, aster, daisy, and coreopsis. As you plan your garden, be sure to include annual flowers as well. Sunflower, marigold, cosmos, cleome, verbena, lantana, zinnia, sanvitalia, geranium, globe amaranth, strawflower, and tithonia are good choices. These easy-to-grow bloomers come in a varied palette that appeals to a wide assortment of animals. Bloom types vary, too, with many species available in both single- and double-flowered forms. Generally, single-flowered types are preferred over double types, but it's a good idea to include a generous helping of both in your garden. To keep your plants blooming all summer, clip off flowers as they fade (until the end of the season, when many seed-eating birds will do your cleanup for you). In milder climates, many of these annual will reseed themselves.

Butterflies seem to prefer the single-flowered 'Signet' marigolds, below, to the more common double varieties. Having a focal point is an important part of garden design. In this garden, opposite, a sundial does more than create interest; it also doubles as a birdbath when it's filled with water. Garden spiders, above, are harmless.

This garden, left, attracts animal visitors because it offers lots of open space surrounded by a food source. White coneflower, right, is drought resistant and popular with insects.

You can expand your yard's wildlife appeal by planting annuals in pots and planters on your patio, porch, or deck. Don't overlook the value of herbs in your wildlife garden either. Many insect species, especially butterfly caterpillars, find herbs a treat. Black swallowtail caterpillars, for example, happily feast on the leaves of parsley, carrot, fennel, and dill. Other herbs you should include are yarrow, mint, chamomile, borage, chive, sweet basil, comfrey, and lavender. With a few exceptions, you can maintain your wildlife flower garden in the same way you care for any flower garden. Avoid use of all chemical pesticides that are harmful to the wildlife you attract. Be less tidy in your garden by allowing a few seedpods to form on faded blooms to provide additional meals for hungry birds. Flowers whose seeds are especially attractive to birds are aster, campanula, coneflower, dianthus, four-o'clock, gaillardia, larkspur, sunflower, marigold, and zinnia. And finally, be sure to mulch your flower garden with several inches of shredded bark, leaves, or pine needles. These materials will do more than just minimize garden maintenance. They'll create a haven for earthworms and other soil organisms that are essential in a healthy garden. These organisms also are an important food source for wildlife.

Coreopsis, opposite, top left, blooms from June through August and attracts a variety of butterflies. In the winter songbirds will harvest the seeds from the faded flowers of this hardy perennial.

Gazania, opposite, far left, is a drought-tolerant annual that produces scores of daisylike blooms right up until frost. It's a favorite food of bees and other flying insects. The flowers close up in late afternoon.

Cleome, opposite, near left, comes in three basic colors: white, pale purple, and violet. Occasionally called spider flower, cleome grows 3 to 4 feet tall. Plant this annual in the back of your flower border.

Globe amaranth, above, offers butterflies a food supply all summer long. It's an easy-to-grow annual that is available in purple, lavender, and white.

CHAPTER THREE

Water Gardens—All animals, whether they fly, creep, hop, or crawl, need water to survive. If you are lucky enough to have a natural body of water, such as a stream or pond, you can increase its wildlife value by adding water and bog plants to the natives already established. If you don't have a natural water source, a man-made pond is just as good. In fact, even if you live on a small lot, you can create a miniature water garden in a large tub or container. The best thing about a water garden is that once it's established, it is relatively maintenance free and quickly becomes a world unto itself, teeming with life of all kinds.

A water garden is the key ingredient to a great wildlife garden

Adding a water source to your garden is easy. First, select a site that receives at least six hours of sunlight a day. Then, decide which type of pool you want to build. There are two popular and easy-to-install ways to construct a water garden. For do-it-yourselfers, you can dig a hole and line it with a plastic liner designed especially for water gardens. Or, you can purchase a preformed plastic or fiberglass pool that sinks directly into your garden soil. Each method has its advantages and disadvantages. Plastic-lined pools offer more flexibility in shape, size, and depth. If you are doing the job yourself, however, it takes time and effort to excavate the pool site. Preformed pools are almost indestructible but come in a limited selection of sizes and shapes that may not look "natural" in your backyard. Check with your garden retailer for advice about the method that best suits your water garden needs. Once your pool is installed, it's important to keep the water fresh, clean, and free of chemicals. Don't contaminate the water by using pesticides, herbicides, or fertilizers nearby. Aquatic animals and plants are particularly sensitive to all of these substances.

Who can resist the sound of water cascading through a garden. This waterfall, left, refreshes both people and wildlife.

To create a complete aquatic habitat, be sure to include each of the four basic types of water plants: oxygenators, bog plants, floating plants, and blooming plants. Keep in mind that a diversely planted water garden will remain clean on its own. Oxygenators grow beneath the surface of the water and compete with algae for food. As their name suggests, these bottom-growing plants add oxygen to the water, which is needed for animals to reside in your pond. Plants that provide oxygen include elodea, milfoil, or cabomba. Floating plants do not require anchored root systems and thrive exclusively on the surface of your pond. Species include duckweed, water hyacinth, and water lettuce.

You don't need a lot of space to enjoy your own water garden. In the halved whiskey barrel, above, an array of water plants grows happily. A preformed sunken pond, opposite, makes a delightful focal point for any garden.

Once you start water gardening, it's easy to become addicted. In this Kansas City backyard, the home-owners turned a large portion of their lot into an aquatic paradise that's a favorite stopping-off place for birds and insects.

Bog plants grow at the edge of your garden and provide cover and living space for a busy world of insects. Bog plants require moist soil and include such species as iris, rushes, cattails, and papyrus. You also can include species that thrive at the water's edge, such as hosta, astilbe, canna lily, and daylily. No pond is complete without blooming plants such as water lilies and lotus. Exotic and mysterious, the adder-headed buds of water lily rise from the water and open in an explosion of bloom. Both water lilies and lotus need to have their roots in soil. Pot these beauties up and set them in the bottom of your pond. By including all four water-plant groups in your garden, you'll have a pond that's well balanced and relatively self-sustaining.

It doesn't take long for a new pond to attract tenants. In this garden, left, frogs moved in right after construction. Box turtles, above, live nearby.

To keep mosquito larvae in check, add some goldfish to your water garden. If you want a more exotic fish species, koi carp are available in a variety of colors. These graceful and friendly fish are delightful to watch swimming among large-leaved water lilies. If your winters are very cold, you should move your garden fish to an indoor tank, or insert a commercially available tank heater into the pond so the water doesn't freeze completely. If you have a deep pond or live in a mild area, these precautions are unnecessary. Among the visitors you can expect to see in your water garden are frogs, toads, turtles, and salamanders. Butterflies and songbirds will also dip in to quench their thirst. You might even coax in neighborhood squirrels, chipmunks, or raccoons. If your pond is large enough, you may find a goose, duck, heron, or egret stopping by for quick snack as well.

Water poppy produces scores of buttercup-yellow flowers, opposite, during midsummer. It can spread rapidly, so be sure to keep it under control if you live where winters are mild.

Meadow Gardens—You don't need a country estate to enjoy a meadow garden filled with the wildflowers and grasses that are common in your area. All you really need is a sunny spot that receives at least six hours of sunlight a day. With careful planning, even a small urban backyard can accommodate the flowers of the field. Many wildflowers, for example, will thrive in large tubs or planters. Once established, a meadow garden requires a minimal amount of work. In fact, one of the best things about a meadow garden is that it eliminates the need to mow your lawn every Saturday morning. Most of all, having a meadow garden is an excellent way to entice wildlife to your backyard.

Consider the flowers of the field for your wildlife garden

Wild meadows are composed mainly of grasses interspersed with a few wildflowers. In your own backyard, you can achieve extra color by adding more wildflowers to the mix. Just remember that grasses are a prolific food source for seed-eating birds and other animals. Although a meadow garden requires more human intervention than it may appear, meadow gardens are easy to sow and maintain. Start with an open location that receives at least six to eight hours of sunlight every day. Most meadow plants will survive infertile soils, but good drainage is important. If your soil is heavy with clay and doesn't drain well, add lots of organic matter to improve drainage. Wet, heavy soil will cause your plants to languish and die. When you start your meadow, don't just scatter seeds and expect instant results. Be patient and keep a close eye on your developing seedlings. It's also wise to include a path or walk through the center of your garden. This will enable you to remove noxious weeds as they appear, especially during the first year, when these aggressive plants will try to get a foothold. Eventually your meadow will be able to take care of itself with less interference from you.

Meadow gardens, right, are a wildlife-pleasing alternative to the traditional bluegrass lawn. Birds and insects will stop by often.

Even in shady areas you can create the look and feel of a sunny meadow. Here, doronicum and other shade lovers create a carpet of color from spring to fall.

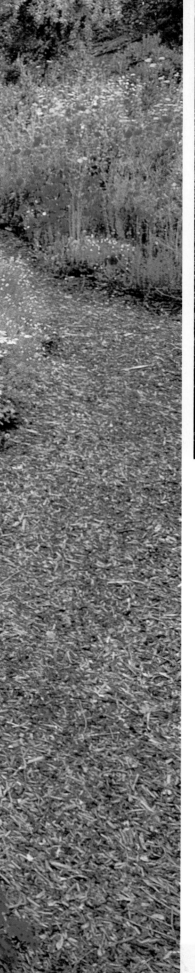

When you plan your meadow garden, select plants native to your area for best results. These plants are accustomed to your climate and are quickly recognized as food by the local wildlife. You can buy seeds of individual species or try premixed combinations sold at your garden center. Beware that some meadow mixes contain plants not hardy in your climate, so be selective when you buy. Some common meadow plants that grow in most regions of the United States include black-eyed Susan, coreopsis, coneflower, aster, sunflower, daisy, goldenrod, and gaillardia. If you create your own blend, select a mix of annuals, biennials, and perennials to ensure all-season color.

Right after planting, a meadow garden, right, doesn't look like much. As the weeks pass, your plants will fill in, above, and eventually pack the bed with flowers of all types, left. Annuals carry the color show the first summer.

Starting a meadow garden

REMOVE WEEDS

RAKE AREA SMOOTH

INSTALL IRRIGATION

SOW SEEDS

Besides the obvious advantage of attracting wildlife to your meadow garden, there's less work for you because you won't have to mow the area. You will have to do a small amount of meadow maintenance, however. As your seedlings develop, pull any coarse weeds that might try to take over the garden. Ragweed, lamb's quarters, and pigweed are three common weeds you'll want to control. You must also cut the area at least once a year, usually at the end of the growing season after the plants have set seed (and after seed-eating birds make their annual harvests). The garden should be cut to a height of 4 to 6 inches. This is best done with a scythe or grass trimmer.

Queen Anne's lace and its relatives, opposite, are common meadow plants across the United States. Part of the carrot family, they're a preferred food plant for a variety of bees and butterflies. They bloom in midsummer.

CHAPTER FIVE

Butterfly Gardens—Flittering from flower to flower, butterflies introduce an added dimension of color and beauty to a wildlife garden. Attracting them to your garden is easy: simply identify the species of butterflies that frequent your area and offer them their favorite foods. Butterflies—and the caterpillars from which they emerge— enjoy feasting on an assortment of perennials and annuals, as well as on nearby native plants and weeds. Many butterfly species may even rely exclusively on plants that you might not consider desirable, such as nettle, clover, plantain, and Queen Anne's lace. Be sure not to use chemical insecticides in your butterfly garden; they often fail to distinguish between butter-flies and other insects.

Butterflies will flock to any garden with a mixed menu of plants

Creating a garden that butterflies find appealing is as easy as planting a packet of flower seeds. Before you start your garden, however, it's a good idea to devote some time to researching the butterflies that are native to your area and their food preferences. Food is the key factor in creating a successful butterfly haven. You need to include a varied menu of flower species that appeal not only to butterflies, but also to the caterpillars from which butterflies emerge. Butterflies feed on the nectar from flowers, shrubs, and vines. Caterpillars, on the other hand, are happy to munch their way through an assortment of leaves, stems, and buds. Adult butterflies will feed on many types of flowers, but caterpillars have a more selective palate and prefer specific plants. The monarch butterfly, for example, happily sips nectar from a variety of bright flowers, but its young eat only the leaves of milkweed. Snout butterflies are another example of a species with specific needs. The adults will feed on any flower, but the young need hackberry leaves.

Butterfly gardens like this one, right, should be located in a sunny spot and include an assortment of colorful plants, such as zinnia, cosmos, blue salvia, strawflower, and pineapple sage.

Caterpillars are voracious eaters and prefer many native plants such as thistle, nettle, clover, wild grasses, Queen Anne's lace, wild lupine, tick trefoil, goldenrod, vetch, and wild aster. Although these wildings can become invasive in a garden setting, it's still a good idea to tuck in a few at the edge of your garden because of their overwhelming value in attracting butterflies. Another place you'll find hungry caterpillars is in your vegetable garden. Carrot, dill, parsley, nasturtium, and fennel are irresistible draws. Butterflies start appearing in your garden as soon as nectar is available—some as early as March. To accommodate these early risers, include spring-blooming shrubs such as lilac, weigela, and witch hazel.

Zebra Longwing butterflies, left, find buddleia flowers irresistible. Nasturtiums, above, are a food plant for many species.

A butterfly favorite, tithonia is an annual flower that grows quickly from seed. The plant grows 3 to 6 feet tall and is smothered in orange-red flowers all summer long. Plant it in the back of your garden.

In addition to native plantings, you can supplement your garden with a dizzying assortment of butterfly food by planting species specifically known for attracting these insects. Butterflies are attracted more by the form of flower than by its color. Generally, butterflies prefer single-petaled flowers, which are rich in nectar and have an area to light on. Fragrant and showy flowers such as peonies or roses often are snubbed by butterflies because their double-petaled form makes nectar-sipping difficult. On the other hand, fast-growing annuals such as zinnia, tithonia, globe amaranth, lantana, dwarf marigold, and cosmos are butterfly favorites. Colorful and nectar filled, these gorgeous blooms are as enticing to human visitors as they are to butterflies. Perennials offer food sources that bloom at different times throughout the spring and summer. Irresistible plant choices are butterfly weed, lavender, coneflower, yarrow, New England aster, and helianthus.

The velvety blooms of 'Black Knight' buddleia, above, belong in every garden. Black swallowtail larvae, right, enjoy parsley, dill, carrot, and fennel.

Once you've satisfied the gastronomic needs of both caterpillars and butterflies, you can attend to some of their other preferences. Butterflies are naturally drawn to sunny areas and are most active when the weather is warm. Don't expect many butterfly visitors in dark, shady locations. If you live in an exposed, windy area, plant your butterfly garden in a protected spot next to a fence, building, or hedge. Like all wildlife, butterflies get thirsty, so don't forget a water source in your butterfly garden. Fill a shallow pan or plate with water, and sink it into your garden soil. When they're not feeding, butterflies like to relax on sun-warmed surfaces. Some butterflies prefer a pan of wet sand to a pan of water. Set a few flat stones around your garden for resting butterflies. If you want to share your garden with butterflies (and other wildlife), always avoid using chemical pesticides. Occasionally some types of butterflies can become pests. The larvae of the white cabbage butterfly, for example, feast on broccoli, cabbage, and cauliflower. To control this species, dust only these crops with bacillus thuringiensis (BT). It's safe for other animals.

New England asters, left, bloom in late summer, just when migrating monarch butterflies, right, need an energy boost.

Even a tiny backyard can attract butterflies. A butterfly retreat was created sucessfully in the Better Homes and Gardens® Test Garden using a mixture of plants to satisfy both adult butterflies and their larvae.

To prove how easy it is to create a butterfly garden, the garden shown here was planted in early May (below) in one of the Better Homes and Gardens test gardens, with species butterflies prefer. By midsummer (left), the garden had completely filled in with a taste-tempting menu of butterfly favorites. The garden plan (right) shows the location and spacing of each group of flowers. Use it as a guide when you plant your own garden.

YELLOW MARVEL MARIGOLDS

BLACK KNIGHT BUDDLEIA

HOLLYHOCKS

BLACK KNIGHT BUDDLEIA

YELLOW NUGGET MARIGOLDS

BORDER BEAUTY ZINNIA

SUN DIAL

PINEAPPLE SAGE

BRIGHT LIGHTS COSMOS

STRAW FLOWER

GLOBE AMARANTH

RED PENTA

WHITE SONATA COSMOS

RED PENTA

LADY-IN-RED SALVIA

YELLOW NUGGET MARIGOLDS

YELLOW NUGGET MARIGOLD

BLUE VICTORIA SALVIA

VARIEGATED LANTANA

RED PLUME GAILLARDIA

VARIEGATED LANTANA

TANGERINE GEM MARIGOLD

PARSLEY

You don't need a lot of yard space to encourage visiting butterflies. You can even lure your favorite species with potted plants on your deck or patio. The lantana and parsley do as well in pots or tubs as they do in the garden.

CHAPTER SIX

Hummingbird Gardens—Darting about in a blur of motion, hummingbirds are the crown jewel of any wildlife garden. Looking more like fairies than birds, hummingbirds are surprisingly easy to attract to your yard. With a craving for nectar and an eye for brightly colored flowers, hummingbirds hone in on nectar-rich blooms with amazing tenacity. Plant a few flowering vines, pot up a flower-filled hanging basket, and post a hummingbird feeder in your yard—you'll have set the banquet table with hummingbird favorites. Hummingbirds aren't the least bit shy. They'll feed on or near a porch, trellis, or arbor where you can enjoy their antics up close. Just be sure to plant the flowers they love.

Invite hummingbirds to your garden with flowers and feeders

Hummingbirds come as close to magic as nature gets: Appearing to hover in midair, their tiny, jewel-toned bodies are kept buoyant by wings beating so fast you can't catch sight of them. Luckily, it doesn't take some magic elixir to entice hummingbirds to your yard. In fact, their palates are quite simple—they have a definite sweet tooth. Although they eat other things, such as small insects, nearly their entire diet is made up of flower nectar. There are two ways to feed hummingbirds: through the plantings in your yard and by setting out specially designed hummingbird feeders. The easiest way to lure hummingbirds to your garden is to plant flowers they are naturally drawn to. Bright-colored blooms in red, orange, and pink are most desirable. Hummingbirds also like bell-shaped blossoms that allow them to dip their slender beaks in for a nectar treat. Many annual and perennial flowers fit their bill of fare. Hummingbird favorites include trumpet vine, fuchsia, and honeysuckle. Other main-course plants include red varieties of impatiens, salvia, petunia, morning glory, and nicotiana. Some hummingbirds also seem to like purple and blue flowers.

Mixed flower gardens, right, are a hummingbird heaven.

To start your hummingbird garden, buy commercially pre-pared seed mixes that contain a mixture of annual flowers hummingbirds feast on. Or, for quicker results, set out bed-ding plants of species hummingbirds crave. In garden beds, it's a good idea to plant brightly colored annuals in masses or drifts. The larger the area of color, the more enticing the bed will be. Hummingbirds also will taste-test flowers in containers, window boxes, and hanging baskets. To attract more hummingbirds, create feeding stations by spreading out the colorful blooms throughout the yard. You also can hang a basket of fuchsia or petunias near your window so you can watch the hungry birds move from blossom to blos-som. Once in your yard, hummingbirds will nest if provided with enough dense foliage for safe cover. Look for their tiny homes in evergreens or deciduous trees and shrubs. In areas east of the Rocky Mountains, watch for the ruby-throated hummingbird, the only species native to this large area. If you live west of the Rockies, you'll have more hummingbird species to enjoy. Different species will share your feeders.

'Lady-in-Red' salvia, left, is one of many annual flowers you can grow to nurture hum-mingbirds. Its red flowers are in full bloom until frost. Other salvia species are also good choices.

Although flower nectar is the natural food of hummingbirds, you can supplement nature's bounty by hanging a hummingbird feeder or two in your yard. Hummingbird feeders are designed to offer what hummingbirds want most: nectar. The "nectar" is actually a mixture of sugar and water (never use honey because it can harm hummingbirds). Most feeders are made of red plastic. You can buy commercially prepared nectar or make your own. Homemade hummingbird nectar consists of four parts water to one part granulated sugar. Mix and heat the solution to dissolve the sugar. Some nectar mixes (and home recipes) suggest adding red food coloring, but if your feeder is red, you don't need to color the nectar. To enjoy a good view of visiting hummingbirds, set your hummingbird feeder near a window or on a patio. Once they become accustomed to your presence, hummingbirds get over their timidness and will come quite close to you. Ideally, you should locate your feeder in a partially shaded spot so the nectar mixture is not exposed to full sun all day. Because the sugar-water mixture slowly ferments as it gets warm, clean your feeder and change the mixture every few days. Other insects, such as bees, wasps, and ants, can cause problems with some types of hummngbird feeders. Be sure to buy a feeder that is designed to keep these intruders at bay. It's also important to hang your feeders high enough to prevent cats from ambushing your winged visitors.

Hanging baskets brimming with flowering fuchsia plants, opposite, will encourage hummingbirds to visit your porch or patio. Pink- and red-flowering varieties of fuchsia are best.

Ruby-throated hummingbirds, left, will visit your garden daily once they discover your generosity.

CHAPTER SEVEN

Housing—Roll out the welcome mat for your favorite forms of wildlife by installing housing designed especially for them. Hole-nesting species such as bluebirds, wrens, chickadees, and purple martins will quickly set up housekeeping if you offer the proper accommodations. Although birdhouses are almost an art form today, birds are more interested in the house's dimensions, size, depth, and entry-hole placement than the color, trim, roofing materials, and other decorative touches. And as any real estate agent will tell you, location is everything, so be sure the location of your wildlife housing meets the needs of the animals you want to attract. The right house in the right place will turn prospective shoppers into neighbors.

Improve the real estate market for your feathered neighbors

Housing size and location are the two key elements in attracting birds to your yard. Just as you would evaluate real estate for your own lifestyle, so do birds. The birdhouses in your yard should be convenient to all the necessities: food, cover, and water. Because different birds have different tastes in housing, however, you need to know about the nesting habits of the species you are trying to attract. Before you build or buy any type of birdhouse, research the wildlife in your area to determine what they are looking for in a home. Find out which hole-nesting species live in your neighborhood and what size house they'll move into. Bluebirds, for example, require a house that is set 4 to 8 feet above the ground in an open area. The house itself should be 5 x 5 inches and 8 inches tall, with a 1½-inch entry hole located 6 inches from the floor. If you mount your bluebird house on a post, add a protective metal collar underneath to prevent raccoons from harassing your guests. Titmice nest in a small house (4 x 4 inches) that is 8 to 10 inches tall. The 1¼-inch entry hole must be 6 to 8 inches from the floor. Mount the box in a wooded setting, preferably from a tree limb about 6 to 12 feet off the ground.

Set purple martin houses, left, in an open area where the birds have room to fly in and out. Paint them white to reflect heat.

Chickadees will move into an empty bluebird box in a minute. Unlike bluebirds, however, they don't like to live in the open, preferring life in a wooded setting. An ideal chickadee house is 4 x 4 inches, with a 1⅛-inch hole located 6 to 8 inches above the floor. Mount chickadee houses 6 to 15 feet above the ground. The natural home for a woodpecker is a hollow tree. Allowing dead trees to remain standing is one way to encourage woodpeckers to move in to your backyard. In lieu of a tree, some woodpecker species will nest in a man-made wooden dwelling. The hairy woodpecker prefers a 6 x 6-inch house that is 14 inches tall and has a 1½- to 2-inch entry hole. A smaller relative, the downy woodpecker, prefers tighter quarters. Its box should be 8 to 10 inches tall with a 4 x 4-inch floor. The 1¼-inch hole should be located 6 to 8 inches from the floor. Position the house in a tree 6 to 20 feet from the ground. Flickers, also members of the woodpecker family, prefer to nest in homes they have created themselves in a dead tree limb. During construction, they will bore out a home that is 12 inches deep with a 3-inch entryway. Without a dead tree, fence post, or telephone pole around for suitable housing, flickers will resort to ready-made housing. Flickers like a floor that measures 7 x 7 inches in a box that is 16 to 18 inches tall. The entry hole should be 3 inches in diameter. Because flickers naturally build their homes in high places, you should locate their house 10 to 20 feet above the ground. Attract larger species such as screech owls, kestrels, and wood ducks to your yard by providing them with appropriate housing designed especially for them.

Wrens aren't fussy about housing. If the entrance hole isn't too large, these tiny birds will readily move into almost any type of house. Both the homemade Japanese-style feeder, left, and the copper-topped, commercial model, opposite, work well.

Wrens are delightful little visitors to your garden. These perky birds consume large quantities of pesky insects, and they are not fussy about the architecture of their home. In fact, wrens will nest in almost any house, regardless of style or color, but it is best to offer them a 1-inch entry hole located an inch below the top of the house. Because wrens prefer small houses, a 4 x 4-inch base is ideal. The box should be 6 to 8 inches tall and located 6 to 10 feet off the ground. Graceful barn swallows skim the air above your garden for mosquitoes, flies, and other insect pests. As their name suggests, barn swallows prefer to build their mud nests in existing structures, like a barn, garage, or porch rafter. Barn swallows are flexible, however, and will readily nest on a man-made shelf tucked under the eaves of a building. Tree swallows will nest in dead trees or bird boxes. They prefer a house that is about 5 x 5 inches and 6 inches tall, with a 1¼-inch entry hole located 1 to 5 inches from the floor of the structure. Tree swallows like to live in open areas near a pond or meadow. Mount the house on a post 10 to 15 feet from the ground. Purple martins, the largest members of the swallow family, like to live in large colonies. Because they are so social, their houses need to be designed with multiple apartments. A house that can accommodate eight or more families is best. Purple martin houses are available in both metal or wood and in a variety of styles, from elaborate to plain. The martins, however, are more interested in the floor plan than the facade. Individual apartments should be 6 x 6 inches with a 2½-inch entry hole. Mount your purple martin house on a pole 15 to 20 feet high and in an open location where the birds can swoop in and out. The houses should be painted white to reflect heat. If possible, include a guard rail to prevent young martins from falling onto the ground. Once a pair of martins adopts your yard as their home, the twosome will return with offspring year after year, multiplying steadily so that you will eventually host a large colony.

Patience is a virtue when you're trying to attract purple martins. If you're lucky, you'll be adopted by a family of martins immediately, but don't give up if the birds fail to show. It may take two or more seasons before the birds decide to move in. The martin houses above and opposite are both mounted correctly in an open, sunny area.

Older birdhouses often h[...]
perch right outside the e[...]
hole. This is not recomm[...]
newer houses because m[...]
orous species may use th[...]
to attack the nestlings. W[...]
bluebirds don't need a pe[...]

When you place birdhouses in your yard, remember that some species are highly territorial. Bluebirds and wrens, for example, will tolerate other species nearby but have a problem with neighbors of their own kind. That's why you shouldn't cluster all your birdhouses in the same tree. Instead, scatter houses throughout the yard, spacing them as far apart as possible. Fall or early winter is the best time to set out birdhouses. By getting your boxes in position then, you'll be sure to entice early spring migrants, and your boxes will have time to weather to a more natural look. Whether you buy or build birdhouses for your yard, look for a design that allows easy cleaning. You should be able to remove a side or top so you can properly clean the box and remove unused nests. During the summer, check the boxes regularly and remove the nests of pest birds like house sparrows and starlings. Checking too often, however, may cause birds to abandon the nest. In the fall, after the last of the young have left the nest, clean out all the old nests and scrub the boxes with soap and water to eliminate any parasites. Bats are another garden visitor that eats insect pests, so attracting them to your garden is a natural way to curb annoying mosquitoes. Because bats are nocturnal, you won't see them during the day. At dusk you may catch a glimpse of one swooping among the tree limbs during their nightly feeding time. Purchase or make your own bat houses to simulate the type of environment bats prefer for sleeping during the day. Bat houses are wooden boxes with a slanted roof and an open bottom where the bats enter. Inside, there are two or more baffles that bats can cling to while they sleep. Hang your bat box on the side of a tree in a clearing in a wooded area.

Bluebird houses, top right, with copper roofs last longer than ordinary models. Bat houses, center right, have an open bottom that the animals use to enter the structure. Screech owl houses, bottom right, should be mounted high in a tree.

Chickadees will be more likely to use a man-made birdhouse if your neighborhood lacks older trees with dead limbs they can nest in. If you live in a heavily wooded area, you may not have much success luring them into birdhouses.

If your yard doesn't have a natural water source, install one or more birdbaths. Birds use baths for both drinking and bathing. Many songbird species will frolic in the shallow waters of a birdbath. Robins, especially, like a good bath. Set your bath in the middle of the garden, with seating nearby so you can observe the antics of bathing birds up close. Once the birds become accustomed to your presence, they will carry on as though you weren't there. Birdbaths come in all shapes and sizes, from elaborate to simple. The birds' requirements are very simple. Whether you buy a birdbath or build your own, make sure it has a sturdy pedestal that won't tip easily. A birdbath should be shallow —no deeper than 2½ inches—so small birds can use it. The edges of the bath should slope gradually downward toward the center so birds can easily scramble out at the first sign of danger. The bottom of the birdbath should be rough enough to give birds adequate footing.

A well-placed birdbath will serve a variety of birds and be an attractive focal point for any style of garden. Concrete birdbaths, right, are a good choice because they won't tip over during storms. Scrub jays, above, are a common sight at Western birdbaths.

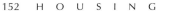

Birdbaths can rest on or above the ground. Raised baths are safer for birds because the added height enables birds to make a quick ascent from ground-stalking garden predators such as cats. Several simple baths set at ground level, however, may entice toads, butterflies, and even an occasional squirrel. If you want to be a really good host, you'll make room for both styles of bath in your garden. To keep birdbaths clean, scrub them once a week with a brush, or give them a thorough hosing. It's also important to keep birdbaths filled at all times all year long. Winter is the season when birds are most in need of water because natural water sources are frozen. Take advantage of the winter's sun by locating baths on the south side of your yard. In areas where temperatures hit freezing for a long period, use a heating source in your birdbath. Many types of electric birdbath heaters are available; some birdbaths even come with a built-in heating coil. If you need to heat your birdbath, move it close to the house to accommodate the electrical cord and for easy maintenance during the winter months. You'll be surprised at how many birds stop in for a drink.

A scrub jay, left, is just one of many species that call this flower-filled oasis home.

Food and Feeders—Supplement nature's pantry by setting out a smorgasbord birds love to eat—suet, sunflower seeds, peanut butter, and other favorite treats. The more varied the menu, the greater variety of bird species you can attract. Feeding birds is not just a winter activity. Keeping the larders full during the rest of the year will encourage birds to move in year-round. Just as each bird species has its favorite foods, each also may prefer a certain type of feeder. Hopper, tube, tray, suet, and fruit feeders are a few of the most popular styles. When you set out feeders of various types around the yard, the local bird population will look to your garden as the place to meet and eat.

Feeding birds can be a year-round activity for the whole family

Although you can feed birds year-round, autumn is the most important time to set out feeders. Migrants will appreciate a free meal on their journey south, while the local bird population will discover early in the season where they can go for a quick snack. As fall slips into winter, native birds will come to depend on your feeders even more, especially after a new snow covers natural food sources. Because birds come to rely on your generosity, it is important to keep your feeders well stocked at all times. Be sure to get your feeders into position before the ground freezes (when the ground is frozen solid, mounting a pole feeder is almost impossible). Place them near shrubs or trees to offer an escape perch nearby. Birds also will feel more at home at your feeders if there is cover. Vary the heights of your feeders to accommodate the feeding needs of different species. Some birds feed on the ground, others are comfortable at tabletop level, and still others prefer eating from hanging feeders. By varying the placement and height of feeders, you'll be able to meet most avian dining preferences. You should continue to feed the birds through the early spring until natural food sources, such as insects and plants, reappear in your yard.

House finches, right, are year-round residents that like a varied menu. They'll eat niger seed, sunflower seed, and seed mixtures.

Blue jays may sometimes dominate feeders and scare off more timid birds. By mounting different types of feeders in various locations, you can keep the jays happy and feed other species, too.

There are nearly as many feeder styles as there are types of feed to fill them. Tray, tube, and hopper feeders are available for seed. For suet, metal cages and mesh bags make a good choice. Each feeder has its advantages. Tray feeders, which should be set on a pedestal or post at least 2 feet off the ground, attract many species because they allow plenty of room for birds to feed together. For the bird-watchers in your household, tray feeders offer an unrestricted view of the birds that come to dine. In bad weather, however, they fill up with rain or snow, making the feed inaccessible when birds need it the most. A tray feeder with a screened bottom will allow water to drain, but you'll need to brush the snow away by hand. Tube feeders are easy to hang and fill and can be stocked with different kinds of seed mixes. Most have several feeding holes with individual perches. Goldfinches will be regular visitors when you serve niger seed (often called thistle seed) in a tube feeder. Although somewhat costly, niger seed is the food of choice for these colorful birds. To minimize waste, use a tube feeder with a catch-tray on the bottom. Tube feeders also are good choices for offering sunflower seed, another songbird favorite. Although several feeders in your yard will increase the variety and number of bird species that visit, if you have room for only one feeder, make it a traditional-style hopper feeder. This feeder design will accommodate the most species and require the least maintenance. Fill your hopper feeder with a basic seed mix. Good mixes will contain up to nine different types of seeds. The more diverse the seed mix, the greater the variety of bird species that will find something to their liking.

Feeders, left, come in assorted shapes, sizes, and styles. During the summer, fruit feeders, opposite, will lure orioles, robins, and other species that don't like to dine on seeds. Replace the fruit frequently.

Sunflower seeds are the favorite food of blue jays, cardinals, chickadees, juncos, nuthatches, and red-bellied woodpeckers. You can buy shelled sunflower seeds, which enable birds to get to the food with less work. Although more expensive than unshelled sunflower seeds, shelled seeds also mean less yard cleanup for you in the spring. Beef suet packed into a mesh basket or onion sack is a preferred winter treat of insect-eating birds such as woodpeckers, flickers, and nuthatches. This high-energy food is available in your grocery store's meat section or from a butcher. Make sure to use *beef* suet. You can maximize its nutritional value by combining the suet with cornmeal, peanut butter, honey, or a seed mix. Attach your suet feeder to the side of a tree or post, or hang it in a tree. Position the feeder about 6 to 8 feet from the ground. Any lower and you may attract

cats, dogs, or raccoons. Keep suet feeders well stocked all winter, but once warm weather arrives, discontinue feeding suet. In the spring, you can continue to feed birds, but you'll need to change your offerings somewhat because natural food sources are available. Instead of seed, offer fresh fruit served in a hollowed grapefruit or orange half for fruit-loving warblers, orioles, and thrushes. Hummingbirds will also stop by when you serve sugar water in a hanging feeder designed especially for them (see Chapter 6, "Hummingbird Gardens").

A corn feeder, opposite, is a good way to feed large birds, such as blue jays and grackles. Squirrels, too, will enjoy a winter picnic of corn-on-the-cob. Post-mounted tube feeders, above, come in a variety of styles, depending on the type of food they're designed for. Besides niger seed, you can offer sunflower seeds, peanut hearts, and safflower seeds.

Woodpeckers, like this downy woodpecker, love beef suet.
Serve it in a suet feeder or a mesh bag. Jays, chickadees,
nuthatches, titmice, and starlings also will stop by for a bite.

While you are celebrating the winter holidays, don't forget to share the season with your outdoor friends. Traditional bird feeders aren't the only way to offer food to overwintering songbirds. You also can feed birds in decorative ways, such as filling a window box with berried and seeded foliage. Choose juniper, holly, wheat or oat shafts, and rose branches loaded with hips to create an edible window-box display. Another holiday touch that will bring rave reviews from visiting birds is a wreath decorated with fresh fruits, vegetables, and other treats. Or make a wreath of bittersweet, pyracantha, or grapevine, all laden with their dried, colorful, and delicious fruit.

In the dead of winter, a vegetable medley hung on a garden gate, left, is a welcome sight to hungry birds. Berry-laden branches tucked into a window box, above, are a colorful repast.

If you're short on space, you can build a multipurpose feeding station like the one at left. This sturdy, easy-to-build feeder has four compartments that hold up to 5 pounds of seed at a time. Well stocked with sunflower seeds, peanuts, or mixed seed, this feeding station will attract lots of hungry birds.

1. Cut the main parts of the feeder from ³/₄-inch exterior plywood. Interior dividers and roof are ¹/₂-inch plywood.

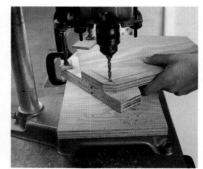

2. Bore the pivot hole in the ends; bore through both end panels at once. Do this by lining them up and clamping them together.

3. Measure and mark out the positions of the ends and dividers on the base. This step saves time during assembly.

4. Transfer divider positions to the ends. Be sure that the ends are dead on their marks as you do this.

5. Glue and nail lattice molding to the bottom piece. Start with the long sides.

6. Mark the end pieces by direct measurement. Butt the piece against one extension and use the other as your marking guide. Glue and nail the end pieces in place, then glue and nail the edgings.

Number	Material	Size (in inches)
2	¾-inch outdoor plywood	17¾ x 21¾
1	¾-inch outdoor plywood	11½ x 20
1	fir	¾ x 3½ x 20
2	fir	¾ x 1½ x 16½
2	fir	¼ x 1½ x 20
3	birch dowel	⅝ (diameter) x 23½
1	glass	⅛ x 17⅜ x 20⅝

7. Bore two shank holes (same size diameter as screw shank) for 2-inch No. 8 screws through both end marks on the feeder base and through marks for the center divider.

8. Trim edging extensions off ends and center the divider with a dovetail saw. Keep the saw blade flush against the adjoining edge and your cut will be flush.

9. Attach ends to the square dividers and the triangular pieces at the bottom of the square dividers. Cut triangular pieces from a 2 x 4. Nail and glue the center.

10. Mount sections on the base, doing the center divider first. Toenail through the center divider into other section. Clamp the gable to each end with pivot holes aligned.

11. Attach roof parts. Glue and nail one side to the gables, then apply glue down the length of the beam of the other roof part. Don't glue to the center divider.

12. Insert a lockpin (use a carriage bolt without a nut) in a hole you bore after painting. Position this hole opposite the pivot pin bolt. Add suet cages to the ends.

CHAPTER NINE

Wildlife Pests—Once you've extended a welcome to the wildlife in your area, you may find some animals less desirable than others. A few bird species, such as starlings and house sparrows, may take unfair advantage of your generosity, especially at winter feeding stations. In fact, these greedy species are known to bully other birds away from feeders. Squirrels, too, are infamous for their bad manners at bird feeders. Depending on the availability of surrounding food sources, your yard may beckon other animals, such as rabbits and deer, which can damage your plants, shrubs, and trees. If you are feeling overrun, take heart—there are many simple and safe evasive tactics you can use to discourage overzealous wildlife.

Keeping unwanted plants and animals from taking over your garden

Squirrels are great fun to watch until they start eating all the feed you've set out for overwintering songbirds. You can discourage squirrels by suspending bird feeders away from overhanging branches. Tube feeders are good choices because they are almost impossible for a squirrel to invade. To squirrel-proof pole-mounted feeders, fasten a metal baffle to the post. Another way to satisfy the gregarious squirrels in your yard is to give them a feeder of their own. Fill a tree-mounted feeder with corn so they'll get their fill and not frequent feeders meant for birds. Many squirrel feeders take advantage of a squirrel's acrobatic skills by incorporating moving parts that twirl the squirrel while it attempts to garner food. The squirrels' antics on moving feeders are great fun to watch. Other pests you'll have to contend with at bird feeders are starlings and English sparrows (house sparrows). These greedy birds are the uninvited guests at every bird-feeding party. To lure them away from feeders, scatter seed on the ground, where they prefer to forage. To discourage sparrows from taking over bluebird and martin houses, remove sparrows' nests every day until they give up and move on.

English sparrows, right, can mob feeders and take over birdhouses.

Probably no animal causes as much controversy as the squirrel. Some people work hard to discourage these furry freeloaders, while others welcome them with corn-on-the-cob and other goodies. It's best to give squirrels a feeder of their own and mount others so they can't take over.

Rabbits won't inhibit your bird-feeding efforts, but they might go after your vegetation. They like to forage on tender twigs, bark, and other plants, and if wild supplies run short, you may find these hungry rodents lunching on your landscaping. To deter rabbits from areas with tender vegetation, erect a wire-mesh fence. To protect individual trees and shrubs, attach plastic tubing or wire mesh around the base of the plant, allowing enough room for future growth. Many commercial rabbit repellents also are available. If rabbits are really hungry, however, repellents may be of little use. Be sure to avoid poisons of any kind in discouraging pests because they can harm the wildlife you want to stay. Sharing your wildlife garden with deer can be a wonderful experience, if the deer populations are moderate. Although these gentle herbivores are indiscriminate grazers preferring buds, shoots, leaves, and tender woody plants, in some parts of the country they are major pests and can clear-cut their way through a garden in a short time. To fence out deer, you need at least an 8-foot barrier because they are agile jumpers. If fencing is impractical, try placing netting over individual garden beds or using a commercial deer repellent. None is foolproof, however.

Sometimes plants can become an even larger problem than birds like English sparrows. Purple lythrum, left, is already creating havoc in many states. Given a foothold, this aggressive bloomer eventually chokes out native species.

Even the most beneficial or beautiful plant can become a pest if it is given the opportunity to grow unchecked. The best rule of thumb is to avoid bringing non-native species to your area—especially if they have the reputation of being rampant spreaders. If in doubt about a particular plant's invasive nature, check with your local nursery or conservation commission before you add it to your garden. Kudzu vine, for example, is a fast-growing perennial introduced to the southeastern United States for use as a ground cover. This aggressive vine, which reaches lengths of 60 feet in one season, escaped cultivation and has now become a major agricultural pest. Multiflora rose was planted extensively for use by wildlife because the plant's impenetrable barrier of thorns makes an excellent "living fence" in pastures and fields. Unfortunately, cattle and other livestock do not browse its thorn-covered branches, and with little to stop it, multiflora rose has literally taken over prime grazing land throughout the country. Porcelain vine is a plant that behaves itself in some parts of the country but grows out of bounds in others. Use it sparingly if you live in an area where this plant proliferates. Lythrum, often called purple loosestrife, is another common garden plant that bears watching. This vigorous species has choked out native plants near streams, lakes, and ponds in Minnesota, Wisconsin, Michigan, and other northern states.

Water hyacinth, right, is a colorful addition to any water garden. Avoid this fast-growing plant in the South, however, because it will squeeze out native plants.

Resources

Organizations

National Audubon Society
700 Broadway
New York, NY 10003

National Wildlife Federation
1400 Sixteenth St., NW
Washington, DC 20036-2266

National Wildflower Research Center
2600 FM 973 North
Austin, TX 78725

Sierra Club
P.O. Box 429005
San Francisco, CA 94142-9848

The Nature Conservancy
1815 North Lynn St.
Arlington, VA 22209

U.S. Fish and Wildlife Serivce
1849 C St., NW, MIB 3012
Washington, DC 20240

World Wildlife Fund
1250 Twenty-fourth St., NW
Washington, DC 20037

Garden Accessories

Bird 'N Hand, Inc.
40 Pearl St.
Framingham, MA 01701

de Van Koek
Dutch Trader
3100 Industrial Ter.
Austin, TX 78759

Droll Yankees, Inc.
Mill Road
Foster, RI 02825

Duncraft Bird Feeders
Penacook, NH 03303

Dutch Trader
3100 Industrial Ter.
Austin, TX 78759

Gardener's Eden
P.O. Box 7307
San Francisco, CA 94120-7307

Gardener's Supply
128 Intervale Rd.
Burlington, VT 05401

Kinsman Company, Inc.
River Road
Point Pleasant, PA 18950

Langenbach
Dept. L9100
P.O. Box 1140
El Segundo, CA 90245-6140

Plow & Hearth
301 Madison Rd.
Orange, VA 22960

Smith & Hawken
25 Corte Madera
Mill Valley, CA 94941

The Nature Company
750 Hearst Ave.
Berkeley, CA 94710

Fruit

Henry Leuthardt Nurseries, Inc.
Montauk Highway, Box 666
East Moriches, Long Island, NY 11940

Miller Nurseries
5060 West Lake Rd.
Canandaigua, NY 14424

Stark Bro's Nurseries
Louisiana, MO 63353

Sonoma Antique Apple Nursery
4395 Westside Rd.
Healdsburg, CA 95448

Flower Seed

Johnny's Selected Seeds
Foss Hill Road
Albion, ME 04910-9731

Park Seed Company
Cokesbury Road
Greenwood, SC 29647-0001

Shepherd's Garden Seeds
6116 Highway 9
Felton, CA 95018

Stokes Seeds
Box 548
Buffalo, NY 14240-0548

The Cook's Garden
Box 535
Londonderry, VT 05148

Thompson & Morgan
P.O. Box 1308
Jackson, NJ 08527

W. Atlee Burpee Co.
300 Park Ave.
Warminster, PA 18974

Perennial Flowers

Carroll Gardens
P.O. Box 310
444 East Main St.
Westminster, MD 21157

Cooley's Gardens
11553 Silverton Rd., NE
P.O. Box 126
Silverton, OR 97381

Gilbert H. Wild & Son
Sarcoxie, MO 64862

Klehm Nursery
Rt. 5, Box 197
Penny Road
South Barrington, IL 60010-9389

Mileager's Gardens
4838 Douglas Ave.
Racine, WI 53402-2498

Schreiner's
3625 Quinaby Rd., NE
Salem, OR 97303-9720

Wayside Gardens
1 Garden Ln.
Hodges, SC 29695-0001

White Flower Farm
Litchfield, CT 06759-0050

Roses

Edmunds' Roses
6235 S.W. Kahle Rd.
Wilsonville, OR 97070

Harrison's Antique & Modern Roses
P.O. Box 527
Canton, MS 39046

Inter-State Nurseries
1800 Hamilton Rd.
Bloomington, IL 61704

Jackson & Perkins
1 Rose Ln.
P.O. Box 1028
Medford, OR 97501

Nor' East Miniature Roses
P.O. Box 307
Rowley, MA 01969

Pickering Nurseries
670 Kingston Rd., Highway 2
Pickering, Ontario, Canada LIV 1A6

The Roseraie At Bayfields
P.O. Box R
Waldoboro, ME 04572

Roses of Thomasville
Thomasville Nurseries, Inc.
P.O. Box 7
Thomasville, GA 31792

Roses of Yesterday and Today
Brown's Valley Road
Watsonville, CA 95076-0398

Bulbs

Dutch Gardens
P.O. Box 200
Adelphia, NJ 07710

Oregon Bulb Farms
Gresham, OR 97030

John Scheepers, Inc.
63 Wall St.
New York, NY 10005

K. Van Bourgondien & Sons, Inc.
245 Farmingdale Rd., Rt. 109
Babylon, NY 11702-0598

P. de Jager & Sons
Box 2010
188 Adbury St.
South Hamilton, MA 01982

Rex Bulb Farms
P.O. Box 774
Port Townsend, WA 98368

Swan Island Dahlias
Box 700
Canby, OR 97013

Wildflowers

Applewood Seed Co.
5380 Vivian St.
Arvada, CO 80002

Clyde Robin Seed Co.
Box 2366
Castro Valley, CA 94546

High Altitude Gardens
P.O. Box 4619
Ketchum, ID 83340

Moon Mountain Wildflowers
P.O. Box 34
Morro Bay, CA 93442

Niche Gardens
1111 Dawson Rd.
Chapel Hill, NC 27516

Vermont Wildflower Farm
Rt. 7, P.O. Box 5
Charlotte, VT 05445-0005

Water Plants

Lilypons Water Gardens
6800 Lilypons Rd.
P.O. Box 10
Lilypons, MD 21717-0010

Scherer & Sons
104 Waterside Dr.
Northport, NY 11768

Slocum Water Gardens
1101 Cypress Gardens Blvd.
Win er Haven, FL 33884-1932

Waterford Gardens
74 EAst Allendale Rd.
Saddle River, NJ 07458

William Tricker, Inc.
7125 Tanglewood Dr.
Independence, OH 44131

Van Ness Water Gardens
2460 North Euclid Ave.
Upland, CA 91786-1199

Garden's Alive!
5100 Schenley Pl.
Lawrenceburg, IN 47025

Necessary Trading Company
One Nature's Way
New Castle, VA 24127-0305

The Natural Gardening Co.
217 San Anselmo Ave.
San Anselmo, CA 94960

Organic Pest Controls

Bountiful Gardens
5798 Ridgewood Rd.
Willits, CA 95490

Gardener's Supply
128 Intervale Rd.
Burlington, VT 05401

Consider your climate

The key to successful gardening is knowing what plants are best suited to your area and when to plant them. This is true for every type of gardening. Climate maps, such as the one opposite, give a good idea of the extremes of temperature by zones. The zone-number listings tell you the coldest temperature a plant typically can endure. By choosing plants best adapted to the different zones, and by planting them a the right time, you will have many more successes.

The climate in your area is a mixture of many different weather patterns: sun, snow, rain, wind, and humidity. To be a good gardener, you should know, on an average, how cold the garden gets in winter, how much rainfall it receives each year, and how hot or dry it becomes in a typical summer. You can obtain this general information from your state agricultural school or your county extension agent. In addition, acquaint yourself with the miniclimates in your neighborhood, based on such factors as wind protection gained from a nearby hill, or humidity and cooling offered by a local lake or river. Then carry the research further by studying the microclimates that characterize your own plot of ground.

Key Points to Keep in Mind:

1. Plants react to exposure. Southern and western exposures are sunnier and warmer than northern or eastern ones. Light conditions vary greatly even in a small yard. Match your plants' needs to the correct exposure.

2. Wind can damage many plants, by either drying the soil or knocking over fragile growth. Protect plants from both summer and winter winds to increase their odds of survival and to save yourself the time and energy of staking plants and watering more frequently.

3. Consider elevation, too, when selecting plants. Cold air sweeps down hills and rests in low areas. These frost pockets are find for some plantings, deadly for others. Plant vegetation that prefers a warmer environment on the top sides of hills, never at the bottom.

4. Use fences, the sides of buildings, shrubs, and trees to your advantage. Watch the play of shadows, the sweep of winds, and the flow of snowdrifts in winter. These varying situations are ideal for some plants, harmful to others. In short, always look for ways to make the most of everything your yard has to offer.

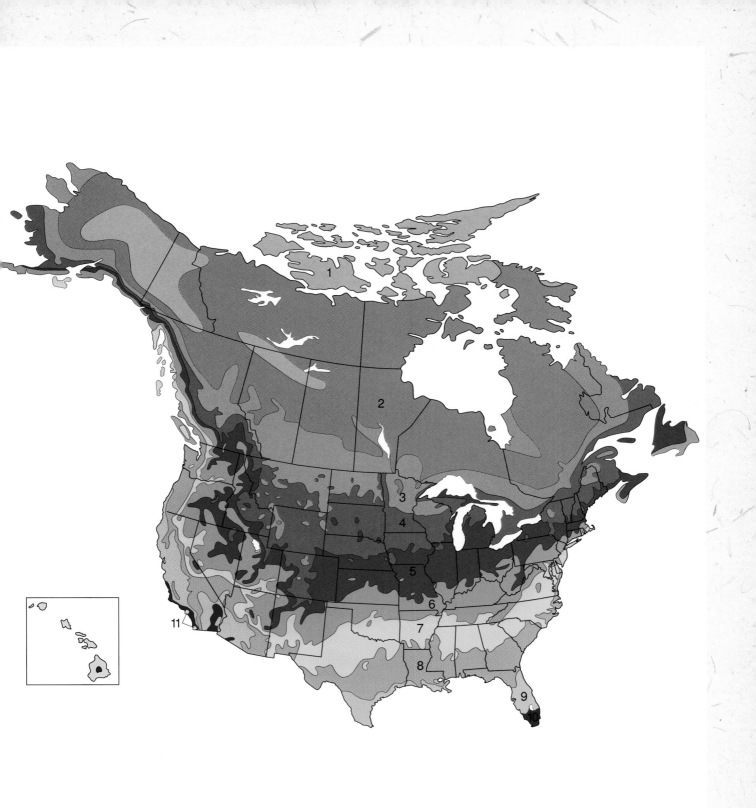

Index